Living Tru
soon comir

Copyright © 2021

All rights reserved. No part of this book may be used or reproduced by any means, graphic, electronic, or mechanical, including photocopying, recording, taping or by any information storage retrieval system without the written permission of the author/ publisher except in the case of brief quotations embodied in critical articles and reviews. The author solely owns the copyrights to the materials herein. Illustrations by anonymous artist.

All Scripture quotations, unless otherwise indicated, are public domain, and taken from the Holy Bible, Authorized King James Version.

Because of the dynamic nature of the Internet, any web addresses or links contained in this book may have changed since publication and may be no longer valid. The views expressed in this work are solely those of the author and do not necessarily reflect the views of the publisher who hereby disclaims any responsibility for them.

Any people depicted in stock imagery provided by Thinstock are models, and such images are being used for illustrative purposes only.
Disclaimer: in the event of any possible adverse actions including misuse of the material by the readers thereof, the publisher and author hereby refuse and deny any and all responsibility of such negligent individuals. The author herein insures that any and all statements made are not made with the intent to harm or discredit any person or their religious beliefs. The sole intent is to present the Biblical view of any and all doctrine. Thus all responsibility for understanding lies solely with the reader.

ISBN: 9798596115765 Library of Congress-in-Publication Data:
An application to register this book has been submitted to the Library of Congres

Living Triumphantly in the soon coming Perfect Storm

Living Triumphantly in the soon coming Perfect Storm

For I the LORD thy God will hold thy right hand, saying unto thee, Fear not; I will help thee. Isaiah 41:13

[12] For our transgressions are multiplied before thee, and our sins testify against us: for our transgressions are with us; and as for our iniquities, we know them; [13] in transgressing and lying against the LORD, and departing away from our God, speaking oppression and revolt,
conceiving and uttering from the heart words of falsehood.
[14] And judgment is turned away backward, and justice standeth afar off:
for truth is fallen in the street, and equity cannot enter. [15] Yea, truth faileth; and he that departeth from evil maketh himself a prey: and the LORD saw it, and it displeased him that there was no judgment. Isaiah 59:12-15.

Living Triumphantly in the soon coming Perfect Storm

Contents

Dedication..5

Introduction...6

Chapter 1 Noah & the 1st *Perfect Storm*...................8

Chapter 2 Not only did Noah survive the 1st *Perfect Storm*...he was Triumphant!............................11

Chapter 3 The Seal of God in the *Perfect Storm*.......13

Chapter 4 Thousands of years to prepare for the 2ND *Perfect Storm*..18

Chapter 5 America's Disillusionment.......................31

Chapter 6 2nd, final and ultimate *Perfect Storm*........35

Chapter 7 The final downsizing...............................39

Chapter 8 Triumphing in the threshing floor.............41

Chapter 9 What to expect in the ultimate *Perfect Storm*..44

Chapter 10 Triumphing as Priests and Kings 1,000 years with the King of kings...50

Chapter 11 Triumphant Wedding Feast....................52

Chapter 12 New Heaven and New Earth...................59

Living Triumphantly in the soon coming Perfect Storm

Glossary……………………..…………………………………..….61

Authors bookshelf……………...…………………………….63

Living Triumphantly in the soon coming Perfect Storm

Dedication

Once again I dedicate this writ to honor my Lord has redeemed me from the slavery of sin to and savior Jesus Christ without whom I am nothing. He walk with Him and talk with Him, changing me as we walk hand in hand.

Living Triumphantly in the soon coming Perfect Storm

Introduction

This is written to instill confidence and faith leading to not only survival but *triumphant* in the soon coming **Perfect Storm.**

It matters not whether you're a pre-trib, post-trib or any other persuasion; the soon coming **Perfect Storm** awaits us all.

Everyone has their *"Personal Storm"* in life from time to time; storms of financial stress, sickness and disease, death, divorce. The list is inexhaustible. **Personal Storms** differ from **Perfect Storms** in that the later is the total destruction of heaven and earth and all that's within it by fire including unrepentant man.

Jesus had his **Perfect Storm** on Calvary 2,000 years ago Perfect Storm. When He died for our sins and the Father forsook him. Yet He arose from the grave and <u>triumphed</u> over sin and death that we might have a new life in him!

In the context of this writ **Perfect Storm** is defined as: the global conditions upon which God's patience, grace and mercy have run out thus making room for His divine wrath and destruction of earth! Scripture records the 1st **Perfect Storm** in the days of Noah for all the exact same reasons as the last and coming **Perfect Storm** in the End Times. Namely extreme wickedness!

Living Triumphantly in the soon coming Perfect Storm

Meteorologists spend hours and days studying weather patterns from snow and rain storms to tropical depressions to category 5 and above hurricanes even predicting/forecasting precise times it will make land fall.

The same goes with the *Perfect Storm.* Precise study of Scripture and current events will produce accurate results in predicting the *Perfect Storm.* This is not a matter of prophecy.

Matthew 24:32-33 says:

32 Now learn a parable of the fig tree; When his branch is yet tender, and putteth forth leaves, ye know that summer is nigh: 33 so likewise ye, when ye shall see all these things, know that it is near, even at the doors. 34 Verily I say unto you, This generation shall not pass, till all these things be fulfilled. So it's not a matter of prophesying, it's a matter of observing the times and circumstances and comparing them with Scripture.

Living Triumphantly in the soon coming Perfect Storm

Chapter 1

Noah and the 1ˢᵗ Perfect Storm

From the outset we're led to believe Noah's *Perfect Storm* lasted just 40 days and 40 nights on the raging high seas! However, upon deeper study we discover Noah and his family stayed afloat in the ark for one (1) year or approximately 370 days counting the 150 days the water covered the earth, the time between loosing the raven and dove then afterward he waited until dry land appeared [the dove sent out the dove signaled it was safe to leave the ark]. Now that is one humongous *Perfect Storm!* Genesis 8:1-22.

Genesis 6:1-12 depicts the global conditions for the
1ˢᵗ *Perfect Storm*

- Wickedness abounding with no restraints on humanity vs.5
- Taking multiple wives vs. 4
- Sons of God/believers took wives of unbelievers

Living Triumphantly in the soon coming Perfect Storm

- Imaginations and intentions, thinking was evil perpetually vs. 5
- Depravity became putrid in God's eyes vs. 11
- World was degenerate, debased, vicious, corrupted in every way vs.12
- In short the 1st *Perfect Storm* fell way short of the 10 Commandments, not as yet given to Moses, Exodus 20:1-17....the first 4 being the vertical relationship between God and man; the 2nd 6 being the horizontal relationship between man and his fellow man.

120 years to prepare for the 1st *Perfect Storm*

God gave man 120 years before the 1st *Perfect Storm*. Noah preached and warned the inhabitants of earth for 120 years before the flood and yet only 8 were saved, Noah, and his family and 2 of every kind of beast and fowl. So also the last and greatest *Perfect Storm* will catch millions unaware because they <u>chose</u> <u>not</u> to obey the gospel although numerous prophets, disciples and believers have given warnings of its impending disaster for thousands of years.

The great differences being:

- The 1st *Perfect Storm* came by a flood.
- The 2nd *Perfect Storm* will be by fire! 2Peter 3:12; Psalm 50:3-4; Isaiah 34:1-4; Micah 1:1-5.

Living Triumphantly in the soon coming Perfect Storm

- Noah wasn't told intricate details of his *Perfect Storm* including how long the *Perfect Storm* would last.
- How much food and fresh water for humans and animals.
- He was told the dimensions and how many animals to gather. Instinctively he provided an ample food supply for both his family and the animals.
- We're not told about provisions for those outside his family or what to do if the limited space was overtaken by outsiders.

The 2nd *Perfect Storm* will culminate by fire [aka ultimate downsizing, more later]

(2Peter 3:10 *But the day of the Lord will come as a thief in the night; in the which the heavens shall pass away with a great noise, and the elements shall melt with fervent heat, the earth also and the works that are therein shall be burned up.*

- Notice: it will include the:
    - ✓ Heavens
    - ✓ A great noise
    - ✓ Elements burnt up
    - ✓ Earth and works will be burnt up

Living Triumphantly in the soon coming Perfect Storm

Chapter 2

Not only did Noah survive the 1st *Perfect Storm*…he was <u>triumphant</u>!

How did Noah triumph?

Noah had only 120 years to prepare for the *Perfect Storm* of his day. Remember the *Perfect Storm* means the destruction of earth.

- Noah not only survived… he was triumphant!
- So exactly how did he triumph?
- ✓ He found favor and grace in God.
- ✓ God was with him.
- ✓ Because God was with him, he refused to panic.
- ✓ Because God was with him on the ark, through the *Perfect Storm* Noah had no reason to fear the storm. He was fearless!
- ✓ He not only heard but also obeyed God voice!
- ✓ Noah started a new life.
- ✓ Noah repopulated the earth.
- ✓ In obedience Noah built an ark/ship according to the exact dimensions, providing food and water for 8

Living Triumphantly in the soon coming Perfect Storm

people and 2 of every kind of animal to last the entire voyage. Modern day cruise ships or war ships are built much larger with plenty of windows, swimming pools, arcades, food courts etcetera. The ark had only one (1(door in front and one (1) window in the top.
- ✓ In patience he and his family waited for nearly a year after the storm ceased, to disembark the ark.
- ✓ Noah thrived not only <u>after</u> the *Perfect Storm* because God was with him through the *Perfect Storm!*

We must remember Satan was on the ark with Noah, as a fallen spirit, so also is he with us:

[8] Be sober, be vigilant; because your adversary the devil, as a roaring lion, walketh about, seeking whom he may devour: 1Peter 5:8

Living Triumphantly in the soon coming Perfect Storm

Chapter 3

The Seal of God in the *Perfect Storm*

We can triumph for God is in the *Perfect Storm* with us

2 Corinthians 1:22

²² who hath also sealed us, and given the earnest of the Spirit in our hearts. (EMPHASIS ADDED)

Ephesians 1:13-14

¹³ in whom ye also trusted, after that ye heard the word of truth, the gospel of your salvation: in whom also after that ye believed, ye were sealed with that holy Spirit of promise,

¹⁴ which is the earnest of our inheritance until the redemption of the purchased possession, unto the praise of his glory. (EMPHASIS ADDED) Contrary to the mark of the beast, which marks for slavery, economic chaos and eternal damnation in the Lake of Fire and brimstone, the seal of the Spirit marks the person with salvation and eternal life.

Revelation 13:16-17

Living Triumphantly in the soon coming Perfect Storm

16 And he causeth all, both small and great, rich and poor, free and bond, to receive a mark in their right hand, or in their foreheads:

17 and that no man might buy or sell, save he that had the mark, or the name of the beast, or the number of his name. (EMPHASIS ADDED) This sounds eerily like communism and socialism aka liberalism. Liberalism carries with it numerous definitions each sounding great but in reality it leads to poverty for common citizens plus implies a certain idea of freedom to "do as one pleases", devoid of regulations. Today I believe America is facing a similar situation in the current presidential election. Literally every country/nation that has endorsed communism and socialism has ended up with the very same economic chaos as depicted here.

Revelation 16:2

2 And the first went, and poured out his vial upon the earth; and there fell a noisome and grievous sore upon the men which had the mark of the beast, and upon them which worshipped his image.

Types of seals

Throughout the Old and New Testaments various types of seals are depicted each with a different purpose. The lesson is to teach:

- ➢ The presence of God.
- ➢ The absolute promise of His promise never to leave you alone.
- ➢ His promise to keep you.
- ➢ His promise to love you
- ➢ His promise to forgive you

Living Triumphantly in the soon coming Perfect Storm

- The ark of Noah was sealed with pitch within and without, sealing out the raging storms, sealing in God's protection, Genesis 6:14.
- ✓ Even though the pitch sealed the ark, yet Satan, the wicked <u>spirit</u> abode within, as evidenced by the events following the disembarkment,
- There was a seal put on the tomb of Jesus to prevent His body being stolen not to mention the soldiers placed to guard it. Matthew 27:62-66.
- The Spirit dwelt in the Tabernacle in the Wilderness fire by night, cloud by day. Psalm 78:14.
- A seal was put over the abyss after Satan was cast in. Revelation 20:3.
- The Holy Spirit was first given to the first believers on the day of Pentecost. Acts 2:1-4. Ephesians 1:13-14.
- The birthright was God's seal of promise as His children. Esau despised it thereby breaking it. Isaac was promised the birthright over Ishmael because of God's promise when Ishmael was the firstborn but to a handmaid.
- 7 sealed book Revelation 5:1-14; 7 sealed book, only the Lamb of God could open.
- Revelation 7 the 144,000 were sealed of Israel and innumerable saints
- Wax seals: 1Kings 21:8; Esther 3:12; Job 14:17; Daniel 2:24.
- Blood seals. Matthew 26:28-30. His covenant seal of forgiveness of sins.

Living Triumphantly in the soon coming Perfect Storm

- Signet rings…on right hand. As a sign or seal of marriage [contemporary], rulers and dignitaries. Genesis 41:42; Numbers 31:50; Esther 3:10.
- Rope seals: 2 Samuel 17:13…a rope that binds.
- The rainbow was God's promise or seal not to destroy the earth by water again, Genesis 5:9-17; The next and last time would be by fire 1 Peter 3:10.
- Seal of the Spirit of promise and down payment of inheritance as first evidenced by speaking in tongues. Acts 2:1-4; 10:44-48.: *[13] in whom ye also trusted, after that ye heard the word of truth, the gospel of your salvation: in whom also after that ye believed, ye were <u>sealed with that holy Spirit of promise</u>, [14] <u>which is the earnest of our inheritance until the redemption of the purchased possession, unto the</u> praise of his glory.* Ephesians 1:13-4. (EMPHASIS ADDED)

These are reminders that even in your personal *Perfect Storm* as well as the ultimate and final *Personal Storm*…He is with you until the end!

- He was with Noah in the ark
- Daniel in the lion's den
- Shadrach, Meshach, Abednego in the burning fiery furnace.
- John on the isle of Patmos
- Peter whet he denied Jesus 3 times
- Abraham on the journey to Canaan Land
- Moses as he led the children of Israel through the wilderness 40 years.

Living Triumphantly in the soon coming Perfect Storm

- God has been with you in every single Perfect Storm in your life!
- And God will be with you in the ultimate, soon coming 2nd and last *Perfect Storm!*

I challenge you to name just one (1) personal storm HE wasn't with you!!!

He will be with you even through the 1st 3 ½ years of the Great Tribulation…the time of Jacob's trouble!

Living Triumphantly in the soon coming Perfect Storm

Chapter 4

Thousands of years to prepare for the 2nd *Perfect Storm*

<u>Remembering once again that, the *Perfect Storm* means God's mercy and grace have run out making room for His divine wrath to destroy the earth and all unbelievers.</u> Nevertheless God is still with us! Grace, love and mercy are the only things holding back God's wrath!

<u>Prelude</u> to the ultimate and final 2nd *Perfect Storm* is detailed as follows:

- The beginning of sorrows, Matthew 24:5-8; Mark 13:6-8; Luke 21: 8-19.
- ✓ Wars & rumors of wars
- ✓ Many deceptive "Christ's"
- ✓ Nation against nation
- ✓ Kingdom against kingdom [yes even in America…at this writing insurrection is happening in the U.S.A as states are contemplating seceding from the Union to become separate nations or co-joined to other states!
- ✓ Famines
- ✓ Earthquakes

Living Triumphantly in the soon coming Perfect Storm

Followed by 7 years called the Great Tribulation/Jacob's trouble

- The 1st half or 3 ½ years, Jacob's trouble will be upon the whole earth (including believers) the final period for believers to warn and invite people to Jesus. It includes persecution, death, jail time etc. all while spreading the gospel and repeated attempts to take the mark of the beast thus cancelling the seal of God…the Holy Spirit [if possible]! God is still with us!

- [God's Wrath isn't poured out until the 2nd half or 3 ½ years of the Great Tribulation Revelation 11:18-19] it's this time that God pours out His wrath upon all unbelievers, those who took the mark of the beast and worshipped him! Tribulation is for everyone while wrath is reserved for unbelievers.

18 And the nations were angry, and thy wrath is come, and the time of the dead, that they should be judged, and that thou couldest give reward unto thy servants the prophets, and to the saints, and them that fear thy name, small and great; and shouldest destroy them which destroy the earth. 19 And the temple of God was opened in heaven, and there was seen in his temple the ark of his testament: and there were lightnings, and voices, and thunderings, and an earthquake, and great hail. I find it curious that while God was calling them to Himself they weren't angry. It wasn't until God's wrath was poured out, after the harvesting/gathering of the saints, that they became angry. Note: the wrath of God lasted 3 ½ years and they begged for death

Living Triumphantly in the soon coming Perfect Storm

but it never came! From the text it's possible that they witnessed the exaltation and rewards of the prophets and those who feared God…believers. Unbelievers don't fear God! There are those today who don't fear God.

- The 1st half will include a one (1) world government thus controlling everyone and everything. Satan is the head of this government, using the Abomination of Desolation, [as an attempt to fulfill his diabolical "5 I wills" in Isaiah 14:13-14 *[13]For thou hast said in thine heart, I will ascend into heaven, I will exalt my throne above the stars of God: I will sit also upon the mount of the congregation in the sides of the north: [14] I will ascend above the heights of the clouds; I will be like the most High.* All this describes Jerusalem, the capital of Israel.

With his ultimate demise: Isaiah 14:15-23.

- *[15]Yet thou shalt be brought down to hell, to the sides of the pit. [16] They that see thee shall narrowly look upon thee, and consider thee, saying, Is this the man that made the earth to tremble, that did shake kingdoms; [17] that made the world as a wilderness, and destroyed the cities thereof; that opened not the house of his prisoners? [18] All the kings of the nations, even all of them, lie in glory, every one in his own house. [19] But thou art cast out of thy grave like an abominable branch, and as the raiment of those that are slain, thrust through with a sword, that go down to the stones of the pit; as a carcase trodden under feet. [20] Thou shalt not be joined with them in burial, because thou hast destroyed thy land, and slain thy people: the seed of evildoers shall never be renowned. [21] Prepare slaughter for his children for the iniquity of their fathers; that*

Living Triumphantly in the soon coming Perfect Storm

*they do not rise, nor possess the land, fill the face of the world with cities.*²² *For I will rise up against them, saith the* LORD *of hosts, and cut off from Babylon the name, and remnant, and son, and nephew, saith the* LORD. ²³ *I will also make it a possession for the bittern, and pools of water: and I will sweep it with the besom of destruction, saith the* LORD *of hosts.* Note: the name, remnant, son and nephew is referring to the descendents of Ishmael also Esau because he married a daughter of Ishmael thereby creating an unbreakable alliance not to war against each other…*a house divided against itself cannot stand.* Mark 3:25…as duly noted in Revelation 13:1-8 *¹And I stood upon the sand of the sea, and saw a beast rise up out of the sea, having seven heads and ten horns, and upon his horns ten crowns, and upon his heads the name of blasphemy. ²And the beast which I saw was like unto a leopard, and his feet were as the feet of a bear, and his mouth as the mouth of a lion: and the dragon gave him his power, and his seat, and great authority. ³And I saw one of his heads as it were wounded to death; and his deadly wound was healed: and all the world wondered after the beast. ⁴And they worshipped the dragon which gave power unto the beast: and they worshipped the beast, saying, Who is like unto the beast? who is able to make war with him ?⁵And there was given unto him a mouth speaking great things and blasphemies; and power was given unto him to continue forty and two months. ⁶And he opened his mouth in blasphemy against God, to blaspheme his name, and his tabernacle, and them that dwell in heaven. ⁷And it was given unto him to make war with the saints, and to overcome them: and power was given him over all kindreds, and tongues, and nations. ⁸And all that dwell upon the earth shall worship him, whose names are not written in the book of life of the Lamb slain from the foundation of the world.*

Living Triumphantly in the soon coming Perfect Storm

Therefore we know the beginning, the duration, the horrific persecutions against the Church and Israel in terms of 7 vials, 7 seals, 7 trumpets, the time of the gathering/harvest aka rapture of the saints/church and the ultimate demise of Satan. All this has been given to the church but Noah had none of this information. He had only to trust the Word of Almighty God!

> - The 1st half or 3 ½ years or <u>Jacob's trouble</u>, Jeremiah 30:7; Daniel 12:1, will bring great distress and persecution upon every believer as we are charged with spreading the gospel until the end of time and the world which is the end of the last 3 ½ years of the Great Tribulation. The Jeremiah passage states that he'll be delivered out of it. So also the Church will be delivered out of it...not from it![the church will go through the 1st 3 ½ years of the Great Tribulation.
> - The <u>2nd</u> half or 3 ½ years will be reserved for all those who refuse the message of the gospel only to be subjected to the Wrath of Almighty God (contrasting or correlating with the flood of Noah's day) while the believers are caught up to heaven in the end time harvest aka rapture.

- Did Noah have to endure the flood? Yes, to begin to repopulate the world.
- Do Christians have to endure the Great Tribulation? Yes!! Because the gospel must be preached to the end of the world (as we know it)!

Living Triumphantly in the soon coming Perfect Storm

The book of Revelation along with numerous Old and New Testament passages outline in great detail the catastrophic events of the last, final and ultimate *Perfect Storm.*

All these passages allude to this event. Notice: <u>they all denote the church being gathered/harvested after the Great Tribulation not before.</u>

Matthew 24:29-31

- *[29] Immediately <u>after</u> the tribulation of those days shall the sun be darkened, and the moon shall not give her light, and the stars shall fall from heaven, and the powers of the heavens shall be shaken: [30] and then shall appear the sign of the Son of man in heaven: and then shall all the tribes of the earth mourn, and they shall see the Son of man coming in the clouds of heaven with power and great glory. [31] And he shall send his angels with a great sound of a trumpet, and they shall gather together his elect from the four winds, from one end of heaven to the other.* (EMPHASIS ADDED)

- 1Corinthians 15:51-52 *[51] Behold, I shew you a mystery; We shall not all sleep, but we shall all be changed, [52] in a moment, in the twinkling of an eye, at the last trump: for the trumpet shall sound, and the dead shall be raised incorruptible, and we shall be changed.*

- Revelation 11:15-17; *[15] And the seventh angel sounded; and there were great voices in heaven, saying, The kingdoms of this world are become the kingdoms of our Lord, and of his Christ; and he shall reign for ever and ever. [16] And the four and twenty elders, which sat before*

Living Triumphantly in the soon coming Perfect Storm

God on their seats, fell upon their faces, and worshipped God, [17] saying, We give thee thanks, O Lord God Almighty, which art, and wast, and art to come; because thou hast taken to thee thy great power, and hast reigned.

- Revelation 12:1-2; *[1]And there appeared a great wonder in heaven; a woman clothed with the sun, and the moon under her feet, and upon her head a crown of twelve stars: [2] and she being with child cried, travailing in birth, and pained to be delivered.*

- *[Travailing in birth and pain to be delivered* are key terms for interpretation], the closer to delivery the more violent the pains/pangs! Deliverance is the key term for such a time as this as it pertains to the delivery of a child from its mother's womb. Revelation 11:15; 12:1-2. This is first spoken of in Genesis 3:15…*in sorrow* [pain] *thalt bring forth children.* The last and final ultimate ***Perfect Storm*** will be violent and painful. Are you ready to triumph in that last and final ***Perfect Storm?*** Remember this is not speaking of the birth of Jesus the Christ…it's speaking of the church being delivered from God's wrath upon the world of unbelievers! Those who refuse the gospel message of salvation through the shed blood of Jesus the Christ.

Birth pangs! Matthew 24:14

[9]Then shall they deliver you up to be afflicted, and shall kill you: and ye shall be hated of all nations for my name's sake. [10] And then shall many be offended, and shall betray one another, and shall hate one another. [11] And many false prophets shall rise, and shall deceive many. [12] And because iniquity shall abound, the love of many shall wax

Living Triumphantly in the soon coming Perfect Storm

cold. ^{13}*But he that shall endure unto the end, the same shall be saved.* ^{14}*And this gospel of the kingdom shall be preached in all the world for a witness unto all nations; and <u>then shall the end come;</u>*

- Deliverance for affliction for the sake of Jesus Christ
- Hated of all nations
- Offences, betrayal and hatred by one another
- False prophets, deception
- Iniquity or wickedness abounding
- The love of many will grow cold
- Endurance to the end = salvation

Birth pangs! Mark 13:10-14

^{9}*But take heed to yourselves: for they shall deliver you up to councils; and in the synagogues ye shall be beaten: and ye shall be brought before rulers and kings for my sake, for a testimony against them.* ^{10}*And the gospel must first be published among all nations.* ^{11}*But when they shall lead you, and deliver you up, take no thought beforehand what ye shall speak, neither do ye premeditate: but whatsoever shall be given you in that hour, that speak ye: for it is not ye that speak, but the Holy Ghost.* ^{12}*Now the brother shall betray the brother to death, and the father the son; and children shall rise up against their parents, and shall cause them to be put to death.* ^{13}*And ye shall be hated of all men for my name's sake: but he that shall endure unto the end, the same shall be saved.* ^{14}*But when ye shall see the abomination of desolation, spoken of by Daniel the prophet, standing where it ought not, (let him that readeth understand,) then let them that be in Judæa flee to the mountains:*

Birth pangs!

- Being delivered to councils, beaten

Living Triumphantly in the soon coming Perfect Storm

- Brought before rulers and kings to testify against them
- Gospel mandate to be preached
- Don't give forethought/premeditate to what you say, the Holy Ghost will tell you what to say
- Brothers will betray one another to be executed; father against son; children against parents
- Hated of all men
- Abomination of desolation standing in the Holy Place

Birth pangs! Luke 21:9-24

⁹But when ye shall hear of wars and commotions, be not terrified: for these things must first come to pass; but the end is not by and by. ¹⁰Then said he unto them, Nation shall rise against nation, and kingdom against kingdom: ¹¹and great earthquakes shall be in divers places, and famines, and pestilences; and fearful sights and great signs shall there be from heaven. ¹²But before all these, they shall lay their hands on you, and persecute you, delivering you up to the synagogues, and into prisons, being brought before kings and rulers for my name's sake. ¹³And it shall turn to you for a testimony. ¹⁴Settle it therefore in your hearts, not to meditate before what ye shall answer: ¹⁵for I will give you a mouth and wisdom, which all your adversaries shall not be able to gainsay nor resist. ¹⁶And ye shall be betrayed both by parents, and brethren, and kinsfolks, and friends; and some of you shall they cause to be put to death. ¹⁷And ye shall be hated of all men for my name's sake. ¹⁸But there shall not an hair of your head perish. To settle it in your heart literally means to be led by the Spirit before, what and when and where and to whom you speak.

This details the 1ˢᵗ half of the Great Tribulation

Living Triumphantly in the soon coming Perfect Storm

[19] In your patience possess ye your souls. [20] And when ye shall see Jerusalem compassed with armies, then know that the desolation thereof is nigh. [21] Then let them which are in Judæa flee to the mountains; and let them which are in the midst of it depart out; and let not them that are in the countries enter thereinto. [22] <u>For these be the days of vengeance,</u> that all things which are written may be fulfilled. [23] But woe unto them that are with child, and to them that give suck, in those days! for there shall be great distress in the land, and wrath upon this people. [24] And they shall fall by the edge of the sword, and shall be led away captive into all nations: and Jerusalem shall be trodden down of the Gentiles, until the times of the Gentiles be fulfilled. (EMPHASIS ADDED) Gentiles are unbelievers persecuting the church and attacking Israel.

Some believe the "days of vengeance" refer to Ishmael's vengeance on Israel/Isaac for attaining the *birthright* which, according to ancient custom, belonged to the *firstborn son* but was given to Isaac as promised by God Almighty 13 years before Isaac was born. In other words Ishmael, and his sons and descendents will exact their vengeance on Israel/Isaac for 3 ½ years before the great wrath of God or *Perfect Storm* is unleashed on all <u>unbelievers</u> which is the main reason for believers to endure the first half or 3 ½ years of the Great Tribulation. The Gentiles refers to all unbelievers in Jesus Christ including Ishmael or Muslims and his followers. Others hold that this is referring to God's wrath in the 2nd 3 ½ years of the Great Tribulation.

Birth pangs!

- Wars & rumors of wars (global)

Living Triumphantly in the soon coming Perfect Storm

- Nation against nation (global)
- Kingdom against kingdom (global)
- Earthquakes, famines, pestilences signs from heaven (global)
- Persecution, incarcerated
- Hated by parents, brothers, relatives

Main location…Israel

- Jerusalem surrounded by armies; why because of Lucifer's 5 "I wills" in Isaiah 14:13-14.
- Those in Judea flee to the mountains
- The days of vengeance (some believe it to be the vengeance of Ishmael while others believe it to be God's vengeance)
- Great distress and wrath
- Many led captive
- Jerusalem trodden down by Gentiles [3 ½ years] (Ishmael is definitely a Gentile [defined as a non-believer in Jehovah God; Ishmael believes in Allah, the moon God]

These 3 passages alone demonstrate the harshness of the very soon coming *Perfect Storm!*

- Just how will you endure?
- How will you survive?
- How will you cope?
- How will you triumph?

Living Triumphantly in the soon coming Perfect Storm

- Noah not only endured...he survived! He not only survived but he coped!
- He not only coped...he <u>was triumphant</u>!
- <u>Noah patiently coped, endured, survived and was triumphant!</u>

Many have already declared the church won't be here...but they've been gravely misinformed. Many also declare the things just mentioned have happened and are irrelevant today. Just as they did in Noah's day! Indeed these things have happened but must come to pass in the End Times and already are thus setting the stage for the last and final *Perfect Storm!*

It's true the disciples experienced quite literally everything in Matthew 24:9...but it's also true that it will happen again...in the last days. The disciples experienced execution, betrayal, jail time, kings and governors charged them and berated them...but that wasn't the *Perfect Storm* we're talking about.

- John the Baptist was beheaded
- Peter was crucified upside down [at his own request]
- The apostle John was exiled to the isle of Patmos where he wrote the book of Revelation.
- Paul & Peter were martyred in Rome circa 66 A.D.
- Andrew was crucified in what is now the Soviet Union
- Thomas was pierced with spears

Living Triumphantly in the soon coming Perfect Storm

- Matthew rumored to have been stabbed to death
- Bartholomew rumored as martyred
- James was stoned and clubbed to death
- On and on the disciples met their own personal *Perfect Storm* but God was still with them!

So, with all that what makes us think we'll be spared the 2nd and final, ultimate *Perfect Storm?*

Are you like Noah prepared not only to survive but to <u>triumph</u> the ultimate *Perfect Storm?*

Living Triumphantly in the soon coming Perfect Storm

Chapter 5

America's Disillusionment

"Contrary to popular belief we don't live in a Christian nation governed by Christian values. In reality America is a secular nation governed by secular laws and the U.S. Constitution which "protects the religious freedoms of virtually every faith or belief system whether Muslim, Christian, Catholic, gay, Transgender, Hindu, or whatever." (Ken Roberts)

"In 1956 Russia's Nikita Khrushchev said Communism would take America without firing a shot; America would implode from within and it without be invaded" (Internet)

I fear the Christian church has become the modern day clone of the 7 churches of Asia Minor by incorporating non Judeo Christian values into its dogma of faith, by supporting various political parties with little or no regard for the Christian integrity of the candidates. Those 7 churches were

Living Triumphantly in the soon coming Perfect Storm

examined <u>and all but one received a scathing review to repent and return to their 1st love, Jesus Christ lest their light be snuffed out. Their religious antics were a bushel dousing their light.</u>

Over the years the church has been duped into believing America is the "Promised Land" when in reality the America we cherish is and always has been a mission field for Jesus Christ, An Oasis if you will, on our journey to heaven, our ultimate Promised Land. To continue on this path will eventually lead to the light/candle being snuffed out just as the 7 churches were warned of. There are plenty of souls in need of salvation. Our task isn't easy nor is it over yet!

Granted we're blessed to have America as out place of nativity, to call our home land and to vote as we should be but for Christians…this is not our Promised Land…we're just passing through on the way to our Promised Land. As Hebrews 1:8 stated: *⁸By faith Abraham, when he was called to go out into a place which he should after receive for an inheritance, obeyed; and he went out, not knowing whither he went.* This is merely a stopping off place or Oasis in the desert, if you will on the way to the Promised Land. Or perhaps better put…<u>a mission field.</u>

As Christians we have 2 nativities:

1. The natural: Jesus said to *render unto Caesar that which is Caesar's* .(Mark 12:17. So we pay taxes to the American government. And we obey the laws of the land insomuch as they don't violate the Laws of God.
2. The new birth or being born again. As Jesus told Nicodemus. John 3:3-8.

Living Triumphantly in the soon coming Perfect Storm

John warns the 7 churches to repent and return to their 1st love in Revelation 2-3. (God was still with them)

There is a grave danger for a Christian in getting <u>overly</u> involved in the politics of any nation to the point where one begins to divide the brethren losing sight of our ultimate Promised Land thereby causing our light/candle to be snuffed out. That's precisely the warning to the 7 churches of Asia Minor, they had religious services under the guise of bushel thus their light was endanger of being snuffed out! The love of God wasn't present! There are churches today with religious pretense hiding under a bushel devoid of the love of and for God! See Matthew 5:14-15.

Unfortunately, loneliness is quite often the result of remaining strong in the faith. For leaders it can prove fatal to a ministry however, Noah remained strong in his convictions of God's instructions, that's exactly what Christian leaders ought to be doing…staying strong in their convictions and teaching those he or she feeds to likewise remain strong in Biblical convictions to…keep the light on<u>. For the Christian one may be lonely but they're never alone.</u>

Matthew 5:14-15 our identity and mission

[14] Ye are the light of the world. A city that is set on an hill cannot be hid. [15] Neither do men light a candle, and put it under a bushel, but on a candlestick; and it giveth light unto all that are in the house.

The gospel is the oil in our lamps both individually and collectively. If we hide our light under the bushel of political

Living Triumphantly in the soon coming Perfect Storm

affiliation then our light is snuffed out and people can't see for they are blind without our light shining brightly in the darkness. It's not that they can't see it's that they have no light to see. Although Noah's light of the gospel shined brightly for 120 years in building the ark yet the people <u>wouldn't</u> see that's why the Church is here…to give light to those who can't see and those who chose not to see…they perish. <u>Be the light! Let it shine! Take it out from under the bushel of politics or whatever!</u>

Stop having "religious programs devoid of the love for Jesus Christ and others in the world which is again akin to putting our light under a bushel! We're not mandated to <u>make people believe</u> only to shine before them. We cannot coerce people into believing, it must be of their own volition. If a person cannot see in the light…how can they be expected to see in darkness? The task of causing belief is the work of the Holy Spirit! Only HE can convict and save!

America has become divided between "us and them" Republicans against Democrats, even in the Church division has permeated it and we hide the gospel under a bushel hiding the light of the gospel. (Madeline Albright, former Secretary of State; Time magazine, February 1, 2021, pg.19.)

Living Triumphantly in the soon coming Perfect Storm

Chapter 6

2nd, final and ultimate Perfect Storm

Once again the 2nd, final and ultimate *Perfect Storm* will include the exact same evil, vile manifestations as the 1st *Perfect Storm* in Noah's day! The only difference I can see is increased wickedness and population!

12 For our transgressions are multiplied before thee, and our sins testify against us: for our transgressions are with us; and as for our iniquities, we know them; 13 in transgressing and lying against the LORD, and departing away from our God, speaking oppression and revolt, conceiving and uttering from the heart words of falsehood. 14 And judgment is turned away backward, and justice standeth afar off: for truth is fallen in the street, and equity cannot enter. 15 Yea, truth faileth; and he that departeth from evil maketh himself a prey: and the LORD saw it, and it displeased him that there was no judgment. Isaiah 59:12-15.

The world is truly getting more and more wicked every day. In 70 ½ years of life I've never heard so many calling and praying for world peace.

It's possible to say the *Perfect Storm* begins with the 1st half of the great Tribulation. On the other hand some

Living Triumphantly in the soon coming Perfect Storm

might declare it begins after the gathering/harvest of the saints. I believe the answer lies in the definition of *Perfect Storm.* Regardless the *Perfect Storm* coming soon and very soon!

The year Noah and his family spent on the ark was the storm magnifying yet protecting them at the same time. When they emerged from the ark on Mt. Ararat they were <u>triumphant</u> despite the *Perfect Storm!* Not just surviving! Life began anew! Yes, Noah endured the loneliness of the loss of friends, perhaps coworkers and relatives who scorned him and most likely so will many of us called to spread the gospel perhaps in obscure ways but nonetheless we're spreading the good word of salvation from the 2nd, final and ultimate *Perfect Storm*! But he was never alone!

Never the less it doesn't come without ample warning! Warning for literally everyone! And the church or believers are still called to preach/broadcast the exact same message…REPENT AND BELIEVE! Repent of your sins and believe the Messiah/Jesus the Christ is here! Trust HIM!

Revelation 6-11 outlines the events of the last and final *Perfect Storm*

7 Seals (vs. 6;10)

- 1st seal thunder, 4 beasts, white horse with bow and crown [nations] (vs. 1-20

Living Triumphantly in the soon coming Perfect Storm

- 2nd seal Red horse with power to take peace from earth and murder one another (vs. 3-4)
- 3rd seal black horse with scale and balances [bringing poverty] (vs 5-6)
- 4th seal pale horse named death and hell had power to kill with the sword, hunger, death (vs. 7-8)
- [saints] slain for their testimony crying to God…How long O Lord; white robes worn (vs. 9-11)
- 6th seal earthquake, sun blackened, moon as blood, stars of heaven fallen dignitaries and common folk hide in rocks from God's approaching wrath (vs. 17-17)

Revelation Chapter 7

- 4 angels on 4 corners of earth holding the 4 winds from blowing (vs. 1)
- Angel from the East with seal of God giving orders not to hurt the earth, sea, trees, 144,000 sealed with God's seal from 12 tribes of Israel (vs. 2-8)
- Great multitude sealed from all peoples, clothed with white robes, giving praise to God (vs. 9-12)
- 7th seal opened, 7 angels given 7 trumpets; prayers of the saints before the throne (vs. 1-5)
- 1st trumpet sounds; hail, blood, fire to burn trees & grass (vs. 7)
- 2nd trumpet sounds; burning mountain cast into sea 1/3 turns to blood, ships destroyed men died for bitter water, (vs. 9-11)

Living Triumphantly in the soon coming Perfect Storm

- 4th trumpet sounds 1/3 of sun smitten/blackout; 1/3 of stars don't shine (vs. 12)
- 5th trumpet sounds; star falls from heaven, bottomless pit opened, swarm of locusts with power as scorpions, forbidden to hurt the grass, or any green thing, tormented 5 months; death evades those who seek it; locusts the shape of horses, crowns of gold, breastplates of iron, tails like scorpions, power to hurt men 5 months (vs. 1-10) all this sounds like the 2nd half or 3 ½ years…the wrath of God. But, through it all…God was still with them, calling them to repentance.[Revelation can be difficult to discern and understand because it doesn't necessarily follow in chronological order, it goes back and forth much like a real life story.]
- One woe is past with 2 more to come (vs. 12)
- 6th trumpet sounds and looses 4 angels 1 month, 1 day, 1 hour to slay 1/3 of the men; 200,000 horsemen still no repentance of wickedness (. 13-21) <u>Note: the 5th, 6th, and 7th trumpets are called woes. All this and still men will not repent!</u> A very sad commentary, and we get upset when someone we know refuses to repent.

<u>All this occurs during the 1st 3 ½ years of the Great tribulation.</u> but through it all God is with us to *triumph!*

Living Triumphantly in the soon coming Perfect Storm

Chapter 7

The final downsizing

From time to time most of us feel the need to downsize. Oh, what a traumatic, disheartening and lengthy experience, to say the least! Few newlyweds move in with a U-Haul full of excess clutter and junk to get rid of. It all creeps in with time, a little here and a little there. Excess socks, jeans, trinkets, nick knacks, gadgets saving junk/stuff for a future time when you "might need it:", before long it all adds up to <u>excessive clutter!</u>

There will come a day when God will downsize everyone regardless of influence, affluence or popularity. In Noah's day the population was severely downsized to 8 people and 2 of every creature to repopulate the earth.

2Peter 3:10

[10] But the day of the Lord will come as a thief in the night; in which the heavens shall pass away with a great noise, and the elements shall melt with fervent heat, the earth also and the works that are therein shall be burned up. Elements; see Glossary. The AMP says "material" which lends itself better to this passage.

Living Triumphantly in the soon coming Perfect Storm

Indeed this is the ultimate downsizing! No more sorting through wanted and unwanted items. No more bickering with yourself; 'shall I keep it or let it go'? Having recently endured such a messy endeavor I know firsthand that when you clean up one closet or space it automatically triggers thoughts of "now what can I put in this empty space???" Literally everything will be burnt up all our prized possessions, homes, cars, bank accounts, the oceans, earth itself whatever you can conjure up will totally be burnt up! To get ready and make room for the New Heaven and Earth…what's more…there won't be an ocean or seas!

Why would God destroy literally everything? After all in Noah's day "everything" wasn't destroyed? Here are some reasons; quite literally everything is polluted.

- The earth is polluted: trash, garbage
- The heavens and planets: man's quests to planets leaving debris
- Ocean: ships, bodies, plastic, trash & garbage from cities using the oceans as a "landfill"[they literally haul their trash on barges built to haul and dump in the oceans.
- Rivers: chemicals, human waste

However, rest assured this will never, ever happen again!

Living Triumphantly in the soon coming Perfect Storm

Chapter 8

Triumphing in the Threshing Floor

The threshing floor, in Scripture, was a place used at harvest time to separate the wheat or grain from the chaff or unusable portion of the crop. In this case harvest time is akin to the wedding feast whereas wedding guests must be prepared, dressed for the occasion and watchful for the bridegroom. Missing either one or both is call for non entry to the feast. See 10 virgins illustration.

Matthew 24:36-51; 25:1-46 alludes to the "threshing floor which appears to occur just before the gathering or harvest of the saints. It will be the time of the 1st 3 ½ years of the Great Tribulation, a time when fathers collide with sons, when families turn against one another. Micah 7:6; Matthew 10:21; Luke 12:52. *For the son dishonoureth the father, the daughter riseth up against her mother, the daughter in law against her mother in law; a man's enemies are the men of his own house.* All this because of the gospel! Yes, it's happening today, however during the 1st 3 ½ years of the Great tribulation things will escalate exponentially. But the true believer will <u>triumph</u> through it all yet still watching while waiting and being prepared and still

Living Triumphantly in the soon coming Perfect Storm

going about their Father's business. It will also be a time when false prophets and false Christ's will run rampant.

Watching & waiting…being prepared

Matthew 24:36-51 admonishes the church to not only attend Sunday and mid week services but to "watch and be prepared for the 2nd advent. Watching and waiting doesn't imply waiting at the bus stop sitting idly by waiting for the bus.

What is implied in the parables is to be busy about your Father's business, doing the "chores", if you will, of the Kingdom. *^{37}Then saith he unto his disciples, The harvest truly is plenteous, but the labourers are few; ^{38}pray ye therefore the Lord of the harvest, that he will send forth labourers into his harvest.* Matthew 9:37-38.

There's still much to be done before He comes again yes, even during the 1st 3 ½ years of the Great Tribulation. We can Triumph! Through great personal tragedy and loss…we can Triumph!

Matthew 25: 1-46 shares several parables to illustrate the dire need for watchfulness and preparedness.

- (Vs. 1-13) are about 10 virgins; 5 wise and 5 foolish waiting for the bridegroom.
- The 5 wise who had plenty of oil in their lamps to light the way at night. Symbolizing both being watchful and prepared.

Living Triumphantly in the soon coming Perfect Storm

- The 5 foolish took no oil for their lamps and ran out having to ask of beg for oil; symbolizing being watchful but unprepared.
- (Vs. 14-30) the parable of the kingdom and the talents illustrating the simple act of using that which has been given to you for the advancement of the Kingdom.
- To withhold your portion no matter how small or large is gross negligence. Too often we fail simple because of jealousy, not feeling worthy or some other excuse.
- (Vs. 31-46) is the parable of the separation of sheep from goats. While in the same family of animals the goat is determined to have its own way and disobedient to the Shepherd's bidding. John 10 3-5 imparts he sheep hear the voice of the Shepherd and obeys. While the goats, in out text, refuses to obey.

The message in the parables is:

1. We, as His sheep, know His voice.
2. As His sheep we need to be obedient to His beckoning; it has nothing to do with "salvation by works" but that of obedience.
3. The harvest is great but the labors are few, Matthew 9:37-38; *[37] Then saith he unto his disciples, The harvest truly is plenteous, but the labourers are few; [38] pray ye therefore the Lord of the harvest, that he will send forth labourers into his harvest.*
4. Reap the consequences whether good or bad.

Living Triumphantly in the soon coming Perfect Storm

Chapter 9

What to expect in the ultimate *Perfect Storm*

The wrath of God

Because Ishmael is the arch enemy of Isaac/Israel he will establish or at least attempt to establish a one (1) world government receiving his power and authority from Lucifer/Satan (during the 1st 3 ½ years). Revelation 13:1-8

[1]And I stood upon the sand of the sea, and saw a beast rise up out of the sea, having seven heads and ten horns, and upon his horns ten crowns, and upon his heads the name of blasphemy. [2]And the beast which I saw was like unto a leopard, and his feet were as the feet of a bear, and his mouth as the mouth of a lion: and the dragon gave him his power, and his seat, and great authority. [3]And I saw one of his heads as it were wounded to death; and his deadly wound was healed: and all the world wondered after the beast. [4]And they worshipped the dragon which gave power unto the beast: and they worshipped the beast, saying, Who is like unto the beast? Who is able to make war with him?

[5]And there was given unto him a mouth speaking great things and blasphemies; and power was given unto him to continue forty and two months. [6]And he opened his mouth in blasphemy against God, to blaspheme his name, and his tabernacle, and them that dwell in

Living Triumphantly in the soon coming Perfect Storm

heaven. <u>⁷And it was given unto him to make war with the saints, and to overcome them: and power was given him over all kindreds, and tongues, and nations.</u> ⁸And all that dwell upon the earth shall worship him, whose names are not written in the book of life of the Lamb slain from the foundation of the world. Revelation 13:1-8. (Emphasis Added) Notice the beast is warring against the saints, you and me.

42 months divided by 12=3 ½ years. Therefore the beast will make war with Israel and the saints 3 ½ years…<u>before</u> the Church and believing Israel are delivered/birthed/gathered/harvested!

- As a one world government, Ishmael/Muslims, being a socialist government, will establish a socialistic government to gain control over the people including the basic necessities of buying and selling Ch. 13:16-17, many times referred to as "a cashless society", thus severely limiting effecting one's ability to even eat. One must have the mark of the beast in their right hand or forehead which some assert to be a micro-chip, symbolizing and sealing their allegiance to the beast/Satan.
- The tenants of Socialism and Communism are very much akin while they may seem desirable and enjoyable their basic tenants are to equally distribute wealth.
- Control society in virtually every aspect essentially leaving them as wards of the state and poverty stricken.
- Public ownership of land and personal property, while this may seem glorious yet it opens wide the

Living Triumphantly in the soon coming Perfect Storm

door to poverty and establish one religion for everyone thereby abolishing multiple religions. Also it leads to anyone occupying your "private" home or business with or without your permission…its public land. With very few exceptions private ownership is eventually non-existent.
- Debasing and rape of women; no longer will they be able to dress and carry themselves as they please.
- Eventually extreme poverty will prevail throughout the world. Every nation converted to Socialism has become impoverished in a very short time frame.
- Socialism & Communism means you're literally at the mercy of such government without a voice.
- An integral part of Socialism/Communism is to reeducate the populace beginning with the youth for the aged are already set against such atrocities. This has been going on for decades, gradually indoctrinating the young minds.
- Defund police, establish marshal law and disarm citizens, except criminals making a "police state" using the military.
- A simple observation of nations converted to socialism and communism will surly reveal this atrocity.
- For the most part all of this and more will happen without firing a shot much like Adolph Hitler being voted into Austria in 1938 by the people, yes even America. (Kitty Werthmann, Holocaust survivor)

Living Triumphantly in the soon coming Perfect Storm

The wrath of God for 3 ½ years

Revelation 15:7-20; 16:1-16; 17:1-18:24

Revelation 15:7-20

This passage outlines those who are to receive the wrath of God. They are those who took the mark of the beast and worshipped him. They made war with the Lamb of God (vs14) ; gave their kingdoms to the beast, they hate the whore (Roman Catholic Church, End Times Study pages 536-537 by Richard Godfrey) This is classic evidence of God's persistent, love for mankind relentlessly pursuing them calling them to repentance and into His fold even during their blatant refusal and wickedness.

Revelation 16:1-16

7 vials of God's <u>wrath</u> poured out by 7 angels.

- 1st angel emptied vial which caused grievous sores (vs. 2)
- 2nd angel vial poured out on the sea which turned to blood (vs. 3)
- 3rd angel poured his vial on the waters and rivers which turned to blood (vs. 4)
- 4th angel's vial poured out on the sun which scorched men but they blasphemed GOD (vs.8-9)
- 5th angel's vial poured darkness on the seat of the beast bringing darkness to his kingdom but they blasphemed GOD refusing to repent. (vs. 10-11)

Living Triumphantly in the soon coming Perfect Storm

- 6th angel's vial poured on the river Euphrates which dried up and produced frogs(vs.12-14)
- 7th angel's vial was poured into the air, a voice from the temple of heaven' throne declared "It is done" and a mighty earthquake shook the earth dividing the city into 3 parts and a great hail storm (vs. 17-21)

Revelation 17:1-18:24

These chapters chronicle the demise of the Mystery Babylon, the Great Mother of Harlots and Abominations of the earth identified as the Roman Catholic Church; its demise and subsequent global financial destruction. (End Times Study by Richard Godfrey pg. 526-547). Some believe the harlot to be the Islamic religion and its worship of Allah, the moon god, and its goal of conquering the world using Socialism, Communism/Marxism. No matter the label one uses the same resulting consequences are undeniable.

Note: that even through 3 ½ years of relentless wrath…God was still there trying to get them to repent…yet they refused!

Mark 4:35-41

[35] And the same day, when the even was come, he saith unto them, Let us pass over unto the other side. [36] And when they had sent away the multitude, they took him even as he was in the ship. And there were also with him other little ships. [37] And there arose a great storm of wind, and the waves beat into the ship, so that it was now full. [38] And he was in the hinder part of the ship, asleep on a pillow: and they awake him, and

Living Triumphantly in the soon coming Perfect Storm

say unto him, Master, carest thou not that we perish? [39] And he arose, and rebuked the wind, and said unto the sea, Peace, be still. And the wind ceased, and there was a great calm. [40] And he said unto them, Why are ye so fearful? how is it that ye have no faith? [41] And they feared exceedingly, and said one to another, What manner of man is this, that even the wind and the sea obey him?

Even in the midst of many Bible passages citing our faith in Jesus I fear the majority on Christians are indeed fearful of going through the Great tribulation having been taught for so long they'd be gathered/harvested beforehand thus not accounting for the faith in Jesus' word He'd be with them through the *Perfect Storm* even as He has been with them in all their personal storms.

Living Triumphantly in the soon coming Perfect Storm

Chapter 10

Triumphing 1,000 Years as kings and priests with the King of kings

After enduring 3 ½ years of Jacob's trouble, being harvested/gathered from the birth pangs and after the 2nd 3 ½ years of God's wrath now it's time to <u>triumph</u> for 1,000 years as priests and kings with Jesus Christ the King of Kings! Note: there are no longer prophets mentioned. Finally He sits upon His throne to reign over the nations for 1,000 years!

Revelation 20:4-6

<u>⁴And I saw thrones, and they sat upon them, and judgment was given unto them: and I saw the souls of them that were beheaded for the witness of Jesus, and for the word of God, and which had not worshipped the beast, neither his image, neither had received his mark upon their foreheads, or in their hands; and they lived and reigned with Christ a thousand years.</u> Note: these are those who came through the Great Tribulation of 3 ½ years known as Jacob's trouble. They kept the seal of the Spirit and dare not take the mark of the beast and worship him. To take the mark of the beast, whatever the mark is, is to renounce your citizenship in

Living Triumphantly in the soon coming Perfect Storm

heaven and as a child of God! It's a dastardly action to say the least!

⁵But the rest of the dead lived not again until the thousand years were finished. This is the first resurrection. Note: these are those who slept or died before the Great Tribulation.

⁶Blessed and holy is he that hath part in the first resurrection: on such the second death hath no power, but they shall be priests of God and of Christ, and shall reign with him a thousand years. (EMPHASIS ADDED)

Clarification: (Vs.4) those reigning with Christ 1,000 years are those who came out of Jacob's trouble of 3 ½ years. They will be priests and kings over the nations reigning in righteousness! They are part of the 1ˢᵗ resurrection.

Clarification: (Vs.5) is referring to those who died before the 3 ½ years of Jacob's trouble.

Living Triumphantly in the soon coming Perfect Storm

Chapter 11

Triumphal Wedding Feast

Revelation 19:1-21

Not much is really said about the Wedding Feast in and of itself. The focus is on the bride and groom with great praise and jubilant rejoicing! The bride's description is that of clean white fine linen…the righteousness of the saints.

The groom is described as riding a white horse, when heaven opens. His name is called Faithful and True. His eyes are like a flame of fire with many crowns. His clothing was dipped in blood. His name is called The Word of God. (vs. 1, 7-8, 11-13)

Because of the sparse description of the wedding feast it's absolutely vital to understand ancient Hebrew weddings.

Ancient and Traditional Hebrew Weddings this all foreshadows and anticipates 2nd coming of Christ

Living Triumphantly in the soon coming Perfect Storm

The father has the final say on matters of marriage.

- Abraham sent his servant, Eliezer, to find a wife for Isaac.
- Jacob, upon falling in love with Rachel and had to work 14 years for her father, Laban [after Laban deceived Jacob] it took 7 years to pay the money owed Laban for Rachel plus 7 more years because the custom was for the eldest, Leah, to marry first. All this was a binding contract.
- This represented an engagement also specifying the man's duties in a contract. A prenuptial contract, if you will.
- Sexual consummation cannot occur until after the wedding.
- Proof of virginity with a cloth on the wedding night. Joseph was minded to divorce Mary when found with child before the wedding. Blood collected from the ruptured hymen on the cloth is the determining factor.
- The wedding feast was a community event whereas the whole town showed up to celebrate the union. Those unprepared were left out when the groom came for his bride. Unprepared meaning they were watching but not adherent to God's Words in terms of obedience. It also pertains to the test of virginity.
- The wedding feast at Cana illustrates this celebration in John 2:1-11 where Jesus turned the water into wine. It also gives understanding of why so much wine was needed.

Living Triumphantly in the soon coming Perfect Storm

[10] "This is what the LORD says: 'You say about this place, "It is a desolate waste, without people or animals." Yet in the towns of Judah and the streets of Jerusalem that are deserted, inhabited by neither people nor animals, there will be heard once more [11] the sounds of joy and gladness, the voices of bride and bridegroom, and the voices of those who bring thank offerings to the house of the LORD, saying, "Give thanks to the LORD Almighty, for the LORD is good; his love endures forever." For I will restore the fortunes of the land as they were before,' says the LORD. Jeremiah 33:10-11.

Commitment, engagement, marriage essential in ancient Hebrew marriages, very similar to Christian practices

- Our Father in heaven sent His son Jesus to obtain a bride…the church
- Jesus was baptized by immersion in the Jordan River by John the Baptist as His spiritual cleansing unto repentance Matthew 3:11.
- The church, bride, individually and voluntarily and willingly is baptized by immersion as its spiritual cleansing. The bride cannot be coerced into marriage. And further baptized by the Spirit. Acts 2:1-1-4 verifying with the Seal/approval, aka earnest of inheritance from the Father thus giving the Father's approval of the bride for His son Jesus.
- As noted before the bride must willingly without force accept the proposal of marriage to the bridegroom.

Living Triumphantly in the soon coming Perfect Storm

- As in Jacob working 14 years for Rachel so also Jesus paid the price for His bride, the church, with His own blood on Calvary.
- The groom, Jesus, then leaves with promise of return, to prepare a place for his bride in His Father's house, John 14:`1-3. The Father's house has many mansions: [Father's house denotes not simply a structure but incorporates the entire family of the Father; the mansions therefore is akin to "abiding" or living; nothing to infer a separate living quarter for each person
- Hence the wedding feast, in reality, more aptly implies the entire church of individual believers. When the bridegroom comes finding them unprepared they are left out. It's an admonishment to be vigilant in watching and preparedness.

"The Lord God said, "It is not good for the man to be alone. I will make a helper suitable for him." Genesis 2:18. It's not good for Jesus to be without a bride.

As the Bride-to-be, we are also asked to be immersed as a testimony of repentance and spiritual cleansing. Note: *[2] and were all baptized unto Moses in the cloud and in the sea;* 1Crinthias10:2.

In Acts 8:26-40 Stephen baptized the Ethiopian eunuch while he was pondering the Messianic prophecy in Isaiah 53:7 and received the gift or seal of the Holy Spirit.

Living Triumphantly in the soon coming Perfect Storm

16 He that believeth and is baptized shall be saved; but he that believeth not shall be damned. Mark 16:16, as we can fully see baptism isn't a fluke, its serious spiritual business.

The betrothal

Whoso findeth a wife findeth a good thing, and obtaineth favour of the LORD. Proverbs 18:2. Not just anyone, the term "wife" refers not to just a female, rather a virtuous woman; Proverbs 31:10-31.
After immersion the couple plans the new household. Sealed with the engagement ring as a contractual obligation on both parts the couple begins to plan.

Matthew 1:18–25 is the example of Joseph discovering Mary, his betrothed, to be pregnant and set out to "put her away, privately" but was stopped by the Holy Ghost. The groom's father has final approval of his bride.

During the time between the engagement and wedding feast the groom is to prepare a place for his bride,

1Let not your heart be troubled: ye believe in God, believe also in me. ² In my Father's house are many mansions: if it were not so, I would have told you. I go to prepare a place for you. ³ And if I go and prepare a place for you, I will come again, and receive you unto myself; that where I am, there ye may be also. John 14:1-3. At this time Jesus is preparing our mansion in the Father's house. Revelation 21:1-2 tells of the "new Jerusalem coning down from God out of heaven prepared as a bride." Note: this bride has all the qualifications of the virtuous woman in Proverbs 31:10-31.

Living Triumphantly in the soon coming Perfect Storm

Only the Father knows exactly when Jesus will return for His bride. She knows only to be prepared and watchful; Matthew 24:36-51. It's always the Father who gives final approval to the marriage.
That brings us to Matthew 25:1-13, the parable of the 10 virgins, 5 wise and 5 foolish.

- 5 were wise watchful and prepared with sufficient oil for their lamps.
- The other 5 were foolish in that they were watchful but took no oil for their lamps.

All this is awaiting the gathering or harvest of the saints at Jesus 2nd coming. Will you and I be found watchful and prepared when He comes?

[6] And at midnight there was a cry made, Behold, the bridegroom cometh; go ye out to meet him. [7] Then all those virgins arose, and trimmed their lamps. Matthew 25:6-7.

[21] Not every one that saith unto me, Lord, Lord, shall enter into the kingdom of heaven; but he that doeth the will of my Father which is in heaven.

The Marriage

[3] And if I go and prepare a place for you, I will come again, and receive you unto myself; that where I am, there ye may be also. John 14:3. At this point is what is normally called the harvest of gathering as in the ingathering if grain. Nissum, Hebrew, which means "to take". Christ is taking His bride home to enjoy the

Living Triumphantly in the soon coming Perfect Storm

wedding feast and live for all eternity. There's overwhelming joy like a "cup the runs over".

Chaste virgin

²For I am jealous over you with godly jealousy: for I have espoused you to one husband, that I may present you as a chaste virgin to Christ. 2Cor.11:2.

Paul's reference to the church at Corinth is in direct reference to the church being found a "chaste virgin" or well disciplined and corrected bride not given to the lusts of the flesh or having worshipped other gods. It pertains to the contemporary church as well.

Scripture tells us "no man knows the hour" but we must remain constantly watching and prepared. He will come <u>suddenly</u> but not imminently or any at time as some insist. Our lives ought to be fully consecrated not "playing the field", so to speak, but wholly given to Him…our Groom!

Living Triumphantly in the soon coming Perfect Storm

Chapter 12

Triumphant in the New Heaven and New Earth

Revelation 21-22

Remember the song: "I can only remember"?

These chapters give us but a glimpse of what Jesus told His disciples: *²in my Father's house are many mansions: if it were not so, I would have told you. I go to prepare a place for you.* John 14:2.

Well here's that mansion Jesus promised!

- Remember that heaven and earth are deceased/passed away they Rest in Peace (RIP). (Vs.1)
- The holy city, New Jerusalem comes down from heaven, as a bride prepared for her husband(Vs,2)
- God is with them [we shall finally see Him face to face] (Vs.3)
- No more tears, dying, pain or suffering, no more death, doctors or hospitals, no more police or military,

Living Triumphantly in the soon coming Perfect Storm

no more memory [amnesia is the only everlasting malady.(Vs.4)
- Water is free. No more monthly water bills! (vs,6)
- (Vs,9-21) describe the bride the Lamb's wife, [a very unique description of a bride I must say] Precious stones of Jasper, Sapphire, Chrysolyte, Chalcedony, Topaz, Beryl, Cryoprasus, Jacintyh, Amethyst, Emerald, Sardonyx, Sardius and streets of Gold. 12 fountains, a city with 12 foundations, 12 gates to the city, huge city is measured.
- God Almighty is the Temple. (Vs.23)

Chapter 22

- (Vs.1-5) River of life, healing for the nations, tree with 12 fruits, no more curse, no night or sun…God is our light.
- At Last we will see the very face of God; no one has ever seen God face to face!
- No evil or wickedness or profane and vile person

We shall TRIUMPH throughout all Eternity!

Living Triumphantly in the soon coming Perfect Storm

Glossary

Capitalism: an economic and political system in which a country's trade and industry are controlled by private owners for profit, rather than by the state.

Elements: base, principle, orderly arrangement, (Strong's Concordance Greek New Testament pg 67; the AMP says "material" thus better lending itself to the passage; NAS says "works").

Perfect Storm: the global conditions upon which due to the wickedness of mankind God's patience, mercy and grace have run out making room for God's divine wrath to destroy the heavens, earth and all substance therein.

Personal storm: includes death, loss, sickness, disease of any and all sorts.

Slept/sleeping: the Biblical definition is death; however Jesus they were sleeping Matthew 9:24; Luke 8:52. Giving the understanding that death is not permanent but would awake in due season.

Socialism syn. Liberalism: most of land is owned by the government and is considered public. Government is in full control; higher taxes; few, if any rights for workers. Sounds great but leads to eventual poverty for the populace in general.   :

Living Triumphantly in the soon coming Perfect Storm

Threshing floor: The threshing floor, in Scripture, was a [lace used at harvest time to separate the wheat or grain from the chaff or unusable portion of the crop.

Living Triumphantly in the soon coming Perfect Storm

Author's Bookshelf

Crossroads of Life Making Tough Decisions Using Biblical Principles, 2011 ISBN 978-4497-2460-3 WestBow Press, Amazon Books

When Lightning Strikes A Time to Mourn a Time to Heal A Study of Grief 2014 ISBN 978-149-4364-786 Amazon Books

Understanding the Christian Birthright A Divinely Inspired, Intricately woven and beautiful Tapestry of the Old and New Testaments 2017 ISBN 978-1511-778-060 Amazon Books

Goliath Slayers A Handbook for Prayer Warriors 2018 ISBN- 13-978-19834-80461 ISBN-10-198-348-0460 Amazon books

Boundaries God's Boundaries bring protection, success and prosperity 2019 ISBN 978179406766

End Times Study A Commentary Peering into the Future ISBN-13: 978-1725728578 ISBN-10: 1725728575

Living Triumphantly in the soon coming Perfect Storm

In the Beginning A Commentary on Genesis
ISBN-13: 978-1725728264

A father's love ISBN: 979-629-336-037

Living Triumphantly in the soon coming Perfect Storm ISBN: 9798596115765

Made in the USA
Las Vegas, NV
26 October 2023